two distinct strands, Brythonic and Goedelic. While Goidelic speakers lived in northern Scotland and Ireland, Brithonic became the significant tongue in Wales and Cornwall. During the period when Roman influence declined and the Anglo-Saxon incursions increased, Brythonic was also spoken in the northern kingdoms of Ystrad Glud (now Strathclyde), Rheged (centred on modern Carlisle) and that of the Gododdin (Edinburgh). Uninterrupted links, both of culture and communications, existed between the people of Wales and these northern Brythonic-speaking peoples until the latter part of the sixth century.

Welsh tradition states that in the fifth century a nobleman called Cunedda Wledig left Manaw Gododdin on the Forth Estuary, settling in Gwynedd in north-west Wales. Having expelled the Irish who had invaded the area, Cunedda founded his own dynasty. His removal to Wales helped maintain links between Wales and the northern kingdoms, even to the extent of soldiers from Gwynedd assisting the men of the north in their attempt to defeat the Saxons at Catraeth.

Cunedda's descendants later ruled in Wales as the royal house of Gwynedd.

In the years after the Roman withdrawal, the main thrust of the barbarian advance was into the north and west of Britain. Saxon victories at Dyrham in Gloucestershire (AD577) and Chester (AD615) effectively isolated the Welsh from other Celtic peoples. When King Offa of Mercia built his famous dyke in the middle of the eighth century – an attempt to define the frontier of Mercia, not

Castell Henllys

effective at keeping out wild animals than any raiding enemy. Hillforts, over 500 of them having been found in Wales, were places of refuge used mainly when danger threatened.

It is sometimes said that the Celts had over 4,000 gods, deities representing elements that were important to primitive people – such as the sea, sky, lakes and stars. The Celtic priests, the Druids, were the only people who could talk to the gods and they held immense power in Celtic society. With no written language, all Druidic knowledge was committed to memory and to enable this to be effective much of it was remembered in verse form. This meant that Druids were often part of the privileged circle of poets and musicians who surrounded the tribal chiefs, praising and lamenting, as required. Only after the victory of Suetonius Paulinus in AD61, when their sacred groves were destroyed, was the power of the Druids finally broken.

One of the consequences of remaining largely independent from Roman influence was that the Celts retained their warlike nature and the legend of King Arthur grew out of this warlike element.

The origins of the legend are now lost but in the sixth century a great Celtic chief and resistance leader certainly existed and it is more than probable that he came out of Wales. The *Mabinogi*, the series of eleven Welsh folk tales that were written down in the fourteenth century but created and recited many years earlier, talk of

Wales – it provided the Welsh, for the first time, with an eastern frontier that stretched nearly 150 miles from north to south. Wales, as an entity, had come into existence.

The Celts lived in family groups, part of widely shifting alliances where community was more important than territory. Tribal chiefs were elected from the noble families and only freemen were given the protection of law. Below the freemen were the unfree and while they were little better than slaves, not allowed to own animals or property, they were the cornerstone of Celtic society. Slaves, on the bottom rung, were valuable because of their economic value. Craftsmen were highly regarded as the men who produced the weapons and decorative metalwork that gave each tribe its standing in society. While men held the top positions in each tribe, noble women were worthy of respect and often exerted considerable influence.

Iron-age Celts lived in round houses with thatched roofs and walls made of wattle and daub. Grouped together inside circular ramparts, they were also protected by a ditch – probably far more

The modern incarnation of the Druids – the Gorsedd of the Bards at the National Eisteddfod.

Cerrig Meibion Arthur (the Stones of the Son of Arthur, North Pembrokeshire).

Caerleon being the site of Arthur's court. There are many other sites with Arthurian connections in Wales, places like St Govan's Chapel in Pembrokeshire (legend states that Govan was actually Sir Gawain) and Castell Dinas Brân in Denbighshire where, it is said, the Holy Grail lies buried. It is all part of the fable. One thing is clear – if Arthur did exist he was not the chivalrous knight of Victorian fiction. He was a Celtic war chief who fought long and hard against the Saxon invaders.

The Gododdin

Y Gododdin is a verse saga written by the poet Aneirin and is an account of the attack by men of the Gododdin on the Saxon-held camp of Catraeth (Catterick) in approximately AD600. Soldiers from Gwynedd joined in the campaign, marching north to join the Gododdin and training for a year before launching their assault. In the face of an overwhelming enemy, the expedition was a complete disaster and the attacking force was wiped out. Only one man, possibly the poet himself, survived. *Y Gododdin* is the earliest major work of literature in the native language of the British Isles – Welsh!

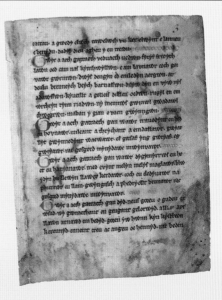

SAINT DAVID AND THE SAINTS

Christianity was brought into the British Isles by the Romans but with the decline of the Roman Empire their embryonic church, its monasteries, abbeys and chapels, came under immediate attack from the pagan Anglo-Saxons.

However, the tradition of monks and holy men withdrawing from the world and living reclusive religious lives remained strong, both in Wales and places like Ireland and Brittany where pagan assaults did not really take hold. This tradition kept Christianity alive during the dark days after the Romans left. From the seventh century onwards a powerful evangelical energy began to flow from Ireland, recently converted by St Patrick, and dozens of wandering missionaries journeyed through Wales, preaching and establishing

Celtic cross at Nevern

centres of learning and prayer. These were the Celtic Saints.

Early Welsh Saints included Dyfrig, the first Abbot of Caldey Island off the Pembrokeshire coast, and Illtud who founded a great monastery at Llantwit Major in the Vale of Glamorgan. Regarded as the 'most learned of the Britons,' Illtud travelled widely in Europe but it is for his monastery, where hundreds came to study poetry, art and rhetoric – as well as the scriptures – that he is best remembered. Deiniol founded a monastery at Bangor in North Wales in the sixth century, as well as a smaller establishment at Bangor-on-Dee but this was destroyed by the Saxons after the Battle of Chester in AD615. St Govan's Church on the cliffs of south Pembrokeshire remains one of the most atmospheric of all early Christian sites.

The stone crosses found in all corners of Wales

St David

These days St David is renowned as the patron Saint of Wales. He died on March 1st, 588 and almost immediately was given hero status, his remains sometimes being carried into battle to ensure success. He was canonised by Pope Callixtus ll in 1120, and it was stated that two visits to St David's Cathedral were the equivalent of one to Rome, three being equal to one trip to Jerusalem.

All over Wales on March 1st, children celebrate St David by dressing in national costume and wearing daffodils. Eisteddfodau, festivals of singing and poetry, are held in schools and by Welsh societies all over the world to mark the day.

are now, in the main, all that remain of the great monasteries of the period. Many of the crosses were originally memorials over graves and were often intricately carved. Examples can be found in Welsh churches – places like Penally, Dyserth and Penmon – and, sometimes, simply standing at the roadside, as with the 13-foot-high cross at Carew in Pembrokeshire. Other good examples exist at Strata Florida Abbey and at Margam.

The influence of the Saints can be seen in the most common of all Welsh placenames, *Llan*. Where their influence was strongest, the evangelists created churches, each surrounded by embankments of earth, marking out religious enclosures known as a *llan*. The term gradually came to refer to a church itself and the word *Llan*, often followed by the Saint's name, can be seen all over Wales in towns like Llanbadarn, Llandeilo and Llanilltyd.

Little is known about David, the greatest of all Welsh Saints. He was born at what is now called St Non's Chapel in Pembrokeshire around the year 520 but most of what we learn about him has its origins in legend and myth.

He established his monastic settlement on the banks of the Alun River where St David's Cathedral stands today. Legend says that Boia, an Irish chieftain in the area, came to throw David and his followers off their land but, for some reason, he could not

St David's Cathedral

fight the holy men, only jeer and call them names. When Boia found all his animals dead in the fields, he realised David had special powers and returned to apologise to him. David brought the animals back to life but tension remained until Boia was killed in battle. The same night a fire came down from heaven and destroyed Boia's settlement.

During his lifetime St David is said to have performed many miracles, in particular sinking wells – important in an age when clean water was a rare commodity – where no water had previously been found. The most famous story about him concerns a time when he preached at Llanddewibrefi. The ground rose beneath his feet so that everyone in the huge crowd could hear him properly.

THE GOOD LAWMAKER

Hywel Dda, his name meaning Hywel 'the Good', was the grandson of another great Welsh ruler, Rhodri Mawr. In the second half of the ninth century, Rhodri had united large portions of Wales under his control and, by strong leadership, limited the incursions of the Saxons for several years. It was a short-lived respite, however. England continued to develop from a land of many kingdoms into one unified state but despite Rhodri's efforts such a situation did not last long in Wales.

When Rhodri died, his lands were divided amongst his six sons and, unable to survive and stand alone, they – along with the rulers of smaller Welsh territories like Dyfed and Gwent – soon declared homage to the English kings. Theoretically, at least, the Welsh people became subjects of the English monarchy.

Hywel Dda became King of Seisyllwg (the modern counties of Ceredigion and Carmarthen) in 900 before obtaining Dyfed by means of marriage and thus creating the kingdom of Deheubarth. In 942 he seized the kingdom of

A page from Hywel's series of laws.

Gwynedd and, later, Powys. Until his death in 949, a large part of Wales was, once again, united under a single ruler and this enabled Hywel to embark upon the process of codifying the customs of the various regions and areas of Wales into a single Law. It is for this series of laws, *Cyfraith Hywel Dda* as they are known, that Hywel is remembered.

According to tradition, representatives from all of Hywel's cantrefs were called to a meeting or convention at his hunting lodge, Tŷ Gwyn in Whitland, on the border of modern-day Carmarthenshire and Pembrokeshire. The exact date of the meeting is unclear but it seems to have taken place over Lent for a period of about six weeks in the late 940s. At this assembly Hywel Dda's Laws were formulated and set down. The old customs were looked at, the useful ones retained, the less useful ones discarded. That, at least, is the legend. Unfortunately, the earliest existing copies of the Laws, eighty Latin and Welsh manuscripts, date from the twelfth century and not all of the information in the books can now be accepted as being entirely accurate.

The manuscripts are copies of the original Laws and two of them, *Gwentian Brut* and *Brut Ieuan Brechfa*, could possibly even have been cobbled together as late as the eighteenth century. All of them contain additions made centuries after Hywel's death. What is certain, however, is that they do contain a considerable amount of material that was written and created during Hywel's reign.

Codification of laws was certainly strong in England at this time and Hywel was on good terms with Alfred the Great of Wessex. Inspired by

Alfred's example he had already taken a pilgrimage to Rome and it is therefore quite conceivable that he undertook the codification of Welsh law with a view to following Alfred's example in England. Quite how deeply Hywel was involved is not now known but certainly Welsh law was codified during his reign and he would have had some share, small or large, in the process.

When Hywel died in 949, Wales once more relapsed into a conglomeration of small, warring kingdoms, threatened by the raiding Norsemen on the one hand and by the power of England on the other. The one thing that did remain, however, was the series of laws that bore the name of Hywel Dda. These laws were used in Wales until the sixteenth century when they were abolished by Henry VIII's Acts of Union. Along with promoting the Welsh language, Hywel's Laws helped foster national spirit in the country at a time when its political independence had all but disappeared.

The Laws of Hywel Dda

Many of Hywel's Laws were enlightened in the extreme. For example, there was to be no punishment for theft, as long as the purpose of the theft was to stay alive – in England children were hung for stealing a lamb until late in the eighteenth century. Under Hywel's laws, compensation for the victim was considered far more important than punishment of the offender.

Precedence was given to a woman's claim in any rape case and marriage

Extract from Hywel's laws at the Hywel Dda Heritage Centre, Whitland.

was regarded as an agreement, not a holy sacrament. Divorce was allowed by common consent, possessions being equally distributed as part of the settlement. Women were given property rights and could even divorce a husband because of his 'stinking breath.' Illegitimate children were given the same rights as legitimate ones and there was equal division of land after the death of a parent.

LORD RHYS, CULTURE AND POWER

The National Eisteddfod of Wales is held every August and attracts thousands of visitors from all over the world, a gathering that extols and celebrates the arts and culture. Yet the Eisteddfod, one of the oldest festivals in Britain, owes its origins to a far bloodier time.

Following the victory of William the Conqueror at Hastings in 1066, Wales lay untroubled for many years. Only in the late eleventh century, when the Marcher Lords of Hereford, Shrewsbury and Chester felt strong enough, were the first incursions made into Wales. What followed was a period of warfare and bloodshed that lasted for several centuries as the invading Normans and Welsh kings and princes clashed in a series of brutal battles for survival.

By 1155 Rhys ap Gruffydd had managed to bring all Deheubarth under his rule and despite being forced, on four occasions, to submit to the power of Henry II, no sooner had the English king withdrawn his troops than Rhys rebelled again. Finally Henry came to terms with Rhys, granting him the title of 'Lord of Ystrad Tywi'. There were to be further campaigns in the years ahead but, for now, Lord Rhys

A commemorative chalice, marking the 800th anniversary of the first eisteddfod.

was sufficiently secure to turn his mind to matters other than warfare.

Rhys was both a proud Welshman and a man of culture. He undoubtedly imitated certain aspects of Norman society but he was careful not to neglect his native Welsh roots – to do so would have alienated those he now ruled. He had a good ear for music and patronised poets who, in their turn, wrote verses in his honour, proclaiming him as a man of power and humility.

In what was probably an effort to display his cultural significance, both to the Normans and to the native Welsh, the Lord Rhys decided to hold a bardic tournament, a music and poetry competition for prizes, over the Christmas period of 1176. Rhys chose to hold the festival not at Dinefwr, traditionally the seat of rulers of Deheubarth, but at the recently refurbished, stone-built castle of Cardigan. This was a significant move as Cardigan had been a Norman borough and only recently acquired from the invaders. It underlined Rhys's achievements in stemming the Norman advance and showed off, wonderfully well, the newly established power of Deheubarth.

Rhys's festival had many of the aspects of the modern event, the eisteddfod being announced a year in advance. Minstrels and bards from places as far flung as England, Ireland and France were invited to come to Cardigan Castle and compete. Two chairs were to be awarded to the victors, one for music, another one for poetry.

A man from Gwynedd in the north of Wales duly won the poetry chair, while a son of Eilon the Crythwr, from Rhys's own court, took the prize for music. Now regarded as the founder of the eisteddfod, Rhys was probably more influenced by similar festivals that had been held in France than by any Welsh traditions. Significantly, no Welsh writer refers to such an event in Wales before 1176 and even the term 'eisteddfod' was not used until the fifteenth century.

Important bardic tournaments continued to be

Stained-glass celebration of the Gorsedd Ceremony at the Ivy Bush Hotel, Carmarthen.

held in the fifteenth and sixteenth centuries but Henry VIII's Acts of Union saw the eisteddfodau decline in significance as Welsh noblemen turned their backs on Welsh culture. Not until the Gorsedd of Bards of the Isle of Britain held a special ceremony at the Ivy Bush Hotel in Carmarthen in 1819, marching in full regalia through the town, did the eisteddfod become a significant force once more in Welsh culture.

Iolo Morganwg and the Modern Eisteddfod

After the Carmarthen ceremony of the Gorsedd in 1819, the eccentric Welsh scholar Iolo Morganwg tried to raise the profile of Welsh culture by claiming the Gorsedd were the guardians of Celtic tradition. The Druidic rituals, he said, were Welsh and he presented documents to prove his claims. Unfortunately they were all forgeries. Iolo's forgeries remained unchallenged until the twentieth century but, by then, the Gorsedd was established as a full and significant part of the Eisteddfod.

The first modern National Eisteddfod in its present form was held at Aberdare in 1860. It now alternates between North and South Wales and has been held every year apart from 1914 and 1940 – when a radio version was broadcast in its place.

LLYWELYN THE GREAT

Dolwyddelan Castle

By the thirteenth century, Wales was dominated by three great principalities – Gwynedd, Powys and Deheubarth. Of these Gwynedd was easily the most powerful and it was from this northern region that the leadership of the Welsh drive for independence was to come.

After a long period of internal strife, by 1199 Llywelyn ap Iorwerth, Llywelyn Fawr as he came to be known, emerged as the ruler of Gwynedd. He immediately drove the Normans back beyond Offa's Dyke, to the very boundaries of Chester,

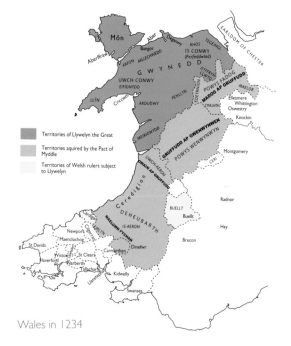

Territories of Llywelyn the Great

Territories aquired by the Pact of Myddle

Territories of Welsh rulers subject to Llywelyn

Wales in 1234

consolidating his position in the north and even making inroads into some regions of Powys. His growing power and military strength were feared by the other Welsh rulers, however, and they supported the English King John in his subsequent invasion of Gwynedd. Llywelyn was forced to submit but as difficulties for John soon arose in England, culminating in the signing of Magna Carta, Llywelyn joined forces with several English barons to attack royal positions and strongpoints in Wales.

Soon, Llywelyn managed to gain the support of several Welsh rulers and set out on a series of campaigns against the English power bases in south-west Wales. He was so successful that in 1204 King John had little option but to recognise him as Lord of Gwynedd. He even gave his illegitimate daughter Joan in marriage to the Welsh ruler. In 1208 Llywelyn conquered the southern part of Powys but his success was beginning to work against him as more and more of the 'petty princes' of the country became fearful for their own independence. John took advantage of this, invaded and forced Llywelyn to agree to humiliating terms.

Such a setback did not last long and, with John clearly aiming at total control of Wales, yet another power shift took place. Those Welsh rulers who had previously aided the English king now fell into line behind Llywelyn to present a united front. John was thwarted in his aims and Llywelyn had clearly become the dominant force in the Welsh military and political spectrum.

At a great council of Welsh rulers at Aberdyfi in 1216, Llywelyn arbitrated on disputes over conquered land and was openly acknowledged as the leader of independent Wales. He began to call himself 'Prince of North Wales'. He would now answer on behalf of all the independent kingdoms of Wales to any external power, thus ensuring that the English King would no longer be able to play off one ruler against the rest.

Strata Florida, site of the Council of Welsh Princes, 1238.

Having spent huge amounts of time and energy building up an extensive and powerful kingdom within Wales, Llywelyn was not about to let it fragment and divide after his death. He sought to ensure the future of his country by replacing the traditional Welsh practice of dividing up inheritance equally amongst all male heirs. Yet he was limited in what he could do. Perhaps almost in desperation, in October 1238 he again summoned the Welsh princes to a council, this time at Strata Florida Abbey. Each of the rulers swore allegiance and undying loyalty to Llywelyn's son and heir, Dafydd.

Knowing the men with whom he was dealing, Llywelyn cannot have felt entirely secure in their assurances.

He was right to worry. The Princes went home from Strata Florida and promptly forgot their vows. In the years ahead it was to be an important factor.

When he died in April 1240, Llywelyn was, effectively Prince of Wales, even though he was content to use only the title of 'Prince of Aberffraw and Lord of Snowdon.' Never again was the country to be so unified or so powerful. Llywelyn the Great, undoubtedly, deserves his accolade.

Llywelyn the Great

For all his pre-eminence amongst Welsh princes, Llywelyn ap Iorwerth never achieved formal recognition from the English crown of his position, power and achievements. When he met the new King Henry lll at Worcester in 1218, he was content to pay homage and hoped that, after his death, Henry would help secure the smooth succession of his son Dafydd. It was not to be. Henry happily played off Dafydd against Gruffudd, Llywelyn's illegitimate son, and managed to confine Dafydd's power to Gwynedd alone.

Henry III

THE LAST PRINCE OF WALES

Dafydd, the son of Llywelyn the Great, died suddenly, without heir, in 1246. His half brother Gruffudd, Llywelyn's illegitimate son, had been killed while trying to escape from the Tower of London two years earlier. That left just Gruffudd's two sons, Owain and Llywelyn, and by the Treaty of Woodstock in 1247 they were forced to agree to a partition of Gwynedd. Henry III took the east of the kingdom, Owain and Llywelyn the west.

Chafing under the humiliating terms of the Treaty of Woodstock, the young Llywelyn first fought against and then imprisoned his brother before declaring himself sole ruler of Gwynedd. He demanded that the lords of Deheubarth and Powys should swear allegiance to him rather than Henry and in 1258 adopted the title 'Prince of Wales'.

Llywelyn's memorial at Cilmeri.

In a series of lightning campaigns, Llywelyn quickly regained eastern Gwynedd and set out on raids that took him deep into Powys and Deheubarth. Taking advantage of Henry's problems with his barons, in June 1265 he sealed a formal alliance with Simon de Montfort, taking de Montfort's daughter Eleanor as his bride. Despite de Montfort's defeat and death at the Battle of Evesham, Henry formally acknowledged Llywelyn's position at the Treaty of Montgomery in 1267 when his title as Prince of Wales was accepted, as was his right to the homage of all the Welsh lords.

Although he, in turn, was expected to pay homage to the English king, Llywelyn had effectively created the Principality of Wales, not through

The Last Prince

There are many legends about the death of Llywelyn. At Aberedw there is a cave cut out of solid rock but with the entrance concealed. Here, it is said, Llywelyn waited for reinforcements that never came. On his way to the cave, with the land under a carpet of snow, the last Prince supposedly reversed the shoes on his horse in order to confuse pursuers. Another tale has Llywelyn fleeing for his life and coming across an old woman. He asks her the name of the stream. 'From now on it is called Nant Llywelyn,' she tells him, 'for this will be your last day alive.'

Whatever the legends, following his death, Llywelyn's head was cut off and sent to Edward at Rhuddlan. The grisly object was displayed for many months at the Tower of London. Llywelyn was buried near to where he fell, a place now called Cefn y Bedd.

military campaigns but as a result of political intrigue and careful diplomacy. For a few years an uneasy peace descended across Wales.

When Henry died in 1272, he was succeeded by his son Edward I. For reasons of his own, reasons that have never been entirely clear, Llywelyn refused to attend his coronation. He was summoned to pay homage to the new king on five occasions between 1274 and 1276. Each time he refused, a deliberate snub that could ultimately have only one result. In 1277, Edward declared war on Wales and invaded.

During the winter of 1276-7, Llywelyn lost much of south-west Wales and the support of many Welsh lords. When Edward advanced, unhindered, along the North Wales coast, the Prince decided to seek terms. The Treaty of Aberconwy in November 1277 saw Llywelyn deprived of all his lands except Gwynedd, west of the Conwy River. He retained his title as Prince of Wales but it meant very little.

For four years relationships between Llywelyn and Edward remained reasonably good although there were regular claims that the King's officials in Gwynedd and Ceredigion were acting in an off-hand and aggressive manner. Then, in March 1282, Llywelyn's brother Dafydd began a rebellion by attacking Hawarden Castle and similar revolts broke out all over Wales. Llywelyn, who realised he had

little choice other than to take part in what was clearly going to be a fight to the finish, joined the rebellion in June.

To begin with the Welsh princes made great headway. Edward's army suffered a heavy defeat at Llandeilo and a seaborne force was decimated while trying to cross to Anglesey over the Menai Strait. It was too good to last. Llywelyn went south, to Builth Wells, to recruit more followers. Reconnoitring English positions on December 11, 1282, shortly after crossing the River Irfon, he was surprised by a small party of mounted English soldiers. In the skirmish Stephen de Francton plunged his lance into the body of an un-armoured Welsh soldier. Only later, when de Francton returned to loot the corpses did he realise he had killed the last Prince of Wales.

A memorial to Gwenllian, daughter of Llywelyn.

Castles of Division and Union

Harlech

Following the death of Llywelyn, his brother Dafydd was left to carry on the hopeless struggle against Edward. Resistance in South Wales quickly collapsed while in the north the King's army marched relentlessly westwards, reaching the Conwy valley and occupying lands as distant as Bangor and Caernarfon. The war began to assume the character of a guerrilla campaign but, with support rapidly falling away, in June 1283 Dafydd was betrayed by his own people. He was subsequently tried for treason and executed at Shrewsbury. With him died all real chances of Welsh independence.

The Statute of Rhuddlan was signed in 1284 and in this document Edward I set out the principles by which he intended to govern his newly acquired territories. It was clear that he was going to rule as an autocratic conqueror. Boroughs on the English style or pattern were created at places like Aberystwyth, Caernarfon and Harlech and the new

Carmarthen

shires of Carmarthen and Cardigan were brought into existence, each of them governed by a sheriff. A system of courts, again in the English style, was set up and English criminal law introduced – including the hue and cry, where inhabitants of towns or villages were duty bound to pursue and, if possible, capture a criminal before he could escape the community limits.

Edward did not attempt to destroy the old Marcher territories along the border. He actually created a number of new Marcher lordships in the north east, places like Chirk, Denbigh and Rhuthun, and gave them to the barons who had helped him in his war against the Welsh. Between the Marcher lordships and the new shires very little of the country actually remained in the direct control of the Crown but it was soon clear that Edward's influence and hand ran strongly in most aspects of Welsh life.

In what was intended to be a 'Royal Procession', the King rode through Wales, his accompanying knights underlining the fact that the English state was the ultimate power in the land. And it was soon clear that the state, using the newly imposed criminal law to end Welsh traditions such as kinsmen investigating and seeking compensation for crimes like murder – often accompanied by vicious and long-lasting blood feuds – would tolerate no deviation. Over the next few centuries came a gradual breaking down of the old Welsh family allegiances or clans – arguably a process that was essential in the development of a modern, unified Welsh nation

Denbigh

Yet Wales could not be subdued and kept under the heel of the English crown simply by the presence of the King and a few new laws. It required military force.

In order to secure his conquered lands, Edward began an ambitious programme of castle building. In South Wales a series of strong, stone-built castles already existed in places such as Caerphilly, Cardiff and, further west, at Pembroke, Carmarthen and Cardigan. These became, along with castles like Dinefwr and Dryslwyn which had previously been held by the Welsh princes, the main economic and military bases in the south of the country.

In the north, however, those areas where Llywelyn's power had been at its strongest, new fortifications had to be built. By 1282 the huge

Dinefwr

stone edifices of Rhuthun, Denbigh, Holt and Hope were already beginning to point their towers and turrets into the air and in the summer of the following year work began on castles at Conwy, Harlech and Caernarfon. Beaumaris, overlooking the Menai Strait on Anglesey, was begun late in 1295, after a sudden uprising under Madog resulted in Caernarfon being temporarily captured. Such a building programme did not come cheaply, however.

By 1301, when most of the work on Edward's new castles had been completed, he had spent over £80,000 on the programme, an incredible sum that would now translate to somewhere in the region of £60,000,000. Stone, lead, iron and timber had been brought to North Wales from all parts of Edward's kingdom and the best craftsmen employed in the creation of the fortresses. James of St George, Master of the King's Works in Wales, was the designer and in places like

Conwy

Caernarfon and Beaumaris he undoubtedly created magnificent castles that were, really, works of art. These concentric castles, powerful, dramatic, each complete with two lines of defence, mark the pinnacle of castle building in Europe.

The castles of Edward I undoubtedly played a major part in the subjugation of the Welsh. They remain, albeit in various stages of ruin and disrepair, as strangely beautiful monuments to the past. Caernarfon, with its polygonal towers and strands of coloured stone; the low, perfectly symmetric lines of Beaumaris; the soaring Round Tower of Flint –

they all retain the power to catch the imagination and the heart of visitors. Yet they were created as units of military power, as the physical manifestation of a totalitarian and dictatorial regime. Without them Edward could never have exercised such a hold over the Welsh people.

The castles and boroughs of Edward's Wales were governed and run by Englishmen, a privileged class who literally changed the face of the country. Welshmen were not allowed to live or trade within castle and borough walls. While there were rebellions and revolts against the incomers, the

Castle building

The earliest castles in Wales were introduced by the Normans. They were a motte-and-bailey design, earth and timber structures consisting of a motte or mound (about 30 feet high) surrounded by a wide bailey or enclosure. Cardiff and Pembroke were both, originally, motte-and-bailey castles that were later re-built in stone.

Chepstow was the first stone castle in Wales, begun by William FitzOsbern in about 1067. The motte element of the early castles remained in the form of, first, rectangular and then circular keeps. The best example of a Round Keep can be seen at Pembroke, inside the original castle, where a 75-foot tower was built by William Marshall in approximately 1200. The concentric castles of Edward I took castle building to new, and hitherto unsurpassed, architectural heights.

Chepstow

system was effective in creating a strong racial superiority amongst the English and marked feelings of inferiority in the Welsh.

Not surprisingly, many of the Welsh lords – the *uchelwyr* – looked on and envied those inside the borough walls. These men hastily tried to win the favour of Edward and his new regime so that what was created was a melting pot of Welshness and rebellion on the one hand, time serving and currying favour on the other. By the fifteenth century, Wales was a hot bed of lawlessness, a place of refuge for outlaws, and although, in effect, the country had been united with England since 1284, in 1536 and 1542 Henry VIII's Acts of Union formally joined the two countries together.

By the terms of the Acts, Welshmen were to have legal equality with the English, the Marcher lordships were abolished and a new series of shires created. Importantly, all judicial proceedings were to be in English and all officials had to be English speaking. It was, in every respect, the logical conclusion of Edward's conquest.

Caernarfon

THE GLYNDŴR REBELLION

O wain Glyndŵr remains a mythical, almost magical figure in Welsh history. In many respects he can be regarded as the Welsh William Wallace, but his rebellion had its origins in a private quarrel between Owain, who could trace his family line to the Royal houses of Powys and Deheubarth, and an Englishman, Lord Grey of Rhuthun.

Tensions between the English and the Welsh had increased during the fourteenth century, a situation that was made worse after 1390 during the general unease in the last years of Richard II's reign. When Lord Grey appropriated some of Glyndŵr's land at Glyndyfrdwy, the Welshman took the matter to law. He was met with the off-hand comment 'What care we for barefoot Welsh dogs.'

Ray Gravell as Glyndŵr.

Glyndŵr captures Rhuthun. (Margaret Jones)

With Grey – tacitly supported by Henry IV, the new English King – accusing Glyndŵr of being a traitor, it was not long before the two men were at each other's throats. The town and castle of Rhuthun were attacked in September 1400 and hundreds flocked to Glyndŵr's standard. Henry unwisely demanded subsidies from the Welsh to fight the rebellion and by the end of 1401 the flames of revolt had ignited across the whole of North Wales. The following year the outbreak spread into central and southern parts of the country.

In the summer of 1403, Glyndŵr and his army swept through Brecon and Carmarthen, English settlers being forced to run for shelter inside their walled towns or castles. That same year he joined forces with Harry Hotspur, the rebellious son of the

The Sleeping Prince

Owain Glyndŵr was not killed in battle, he simply disappeared. Nowadays it is reasonably sure that he died peacefully in Herefordshire, at the home of the Scudamore family, in 1415 when he was sixty years of age and all thoughts of rebellion had long since passed.

For the bards and singers of Wales, however, his disappearance was too good a chance to miss. Glyndŵr was, they said, not dead, simply sleeping in a cave with his best warriors, waiting to be awakened when Wales had need of him again. When Henry Tudor defeated Richard lll at the Battle of Bosworth Field in 1485 to become Henry Vll, many believed that Glyndŵr had awoken and returned to seize his rightful inheritance.

LAWS AGAINST THE WELSH

In March 1401, in response to vociferous protests against the Welsh in Parliament, the king passed harsh new laws.

- It was illegal for any Englishman to be prosecuted in Wales by a Welshman. An Englishman had to be found to conduct the hearing.
- Bards were forbidden to sustain themselves by minstrelsy.
- Welshmen were forbidden to hold any meetings without having a representative of the crown present
- No Welshman unless he were a bishop or a temporal lord, could possess a castle or defend his house.
- No Welshman was allowed to hold a responsible post.
- No Englishman, if he were married to a Welsh woman, was allowed to hold a responsible post in Wales or the Marches.
- Welshmen were not allowed to carry arms without a special licence.
- No food or armour was to be sent into Wales and an English official was appointed to stop supplies.
- All garrisons and walled towns were to be manned by Englishmen.

Earl of Northumberland, and received military aid from French and Breton forces.

In 1404 he captured Harlech and Aberystwyth castles and summoned a parliament at Machynlleth where he was crowned Prince of Wales in the presence of envoys from Scotland, Spain and France. The summoning of Glyndŵr's Parliament was a seminal moment in the history of Wales but the country would have to wait a further 600 years to host another such assembly. For Owain Glyndŵr this was the summit of his success. He now controlled virtually the whole of Wales and the English administration of the Principality almost ground to a halt. Rents could not be collected for fear of Glyndŵr and courts were unable to sit. The new Prince of Wales even signed an agreement with the French King to make the Welsh church subject to the Pope at Avignon, rather than the one in Rome. Then it all began to go wrong.

Early in 1405, Glyndŵr, along with the Earl of Northumberland and Edmund Mortimer, signed the idealistic (and unrealistic) Tripartite Indenture, an agreement that planned to defeat and remove Henry and divide the kingdom into three. Glyndŵr was to hold Wales and the border country. The resulting Welsh invasion of England, supported by a French army that had landed in Milford Haven, ended in failure as Glyndŵr, with no lines of supply, had little option but to retreat back beyond Offa's Dyke. Prince Harry, later King Henry V, called off the pursuit in the face of freezing weather, the dreadful conditions being blamed on Glyndŵr's supernatural powers.

After this, Glyndŵr was constantly on the back foot, fighting rearguard actions, trying to counter the growing military skill of the young Prince Hal. All but one of his six sons were killed in skirmishes with the English, his alliance with France collapsed in 1407 and by 1410 the rebellion had simply petered out.

Owain Glyndŵr's fight for independence was, ultimately, a failure. Yet he had given heart to his fellow countrymen in what was the last element of resistance against the English overlords, a resistance that had begun more than a hundred years before.

Celebrating the 600th anniversary of Glyndŵr's parliament, Machynlleth 2004.

THE PEOPLE'S BIBLE

Whatever the motives behind Henry VIII's Reformation in the 1530s, the break with the Church of Rome was a far-reaching and highly significant event. Yet it was not something that happened without objection or dispute.

As far as the people of Wales were concerned, it was a settlement that was forced upon them and when the Book of Common Prayer was introduced during the reign of Henry's son, Edward VI, the replacement of Latin rituals by English ones did little to make Welsh church services more welcoming. Most Welsh men and women could no more understand the English words than they could the Latin – but at least the old Catholic services had been familiar.

The security of Wales was important to the Tudors as it was the logical place for any invading army to land. Henry VII himself had come ashore near Milford Haven and his grand-daughter Queen Elizabeth, at bay and excommunicated by

Llanrhaeadr-ym-Mochnant

the Pope, knew how important it was to keep Wales calm and at peace. Consequently, in an Act of Parliament passed in 1563, the Welsh Bishops were commanded to allow the translation of the Bible and the Book of Common Prayer into Welsh because 'the English tongue is not understood by the greatest number of Her Majesty's obedient subjects inhabiting Wales.'

The first translations of the New Testament and Book of Prayer appeared in 1567. They were the work of William Salesbury, a Welsh lawyer from Denbigh who had been educated at Oxford but retained a great love of the Welsh language. Salesbury's odd prose style did little to endear itself to the Welsh congregations and he died in 1584 without having produced the translation of the Old Testament, as had been originally intended.

William Morgan was born in 1545, the son of a tenant farmer on the Gwydir Estates, Nant Conwy. Educated at Cambridge, he became the vicar of Llanrhaeadr-ym-Mochnant in 1578 and, realising the inadequacies of Salesbury's work, spent the next ten years making a full translation of the Bible into Welsh. He was encouraged and financially supported in his work by no less a person than Archbishop Whitgift and was helped by the scholar John Davies and poet Edmwnd Prys. Morgan's Bible appeared in 1588.

What Morgan produced was a Welsh literary classic, a work of stunning beauty that was linguistically accurate, appealing to the labourer and gentry alike. It has been claimed that Morgan's Bible saved the Welsh language from extinction, a claim that can be readily substantiated.

At the end of the sixteenth century, there was considerable decay in the Welsh language which

The new 1988 translation of the Welsh bible.

was beginning to split and fragment into a number of different dialects, idioms and styles. Morgan went back to sources such as the *Mabinogi* and early bardic poems to escape the current corruption of the Welsh tongue. What he produced was a Bible with great purity of language, whose lyrical, flowing style took up where the great bardic poems of the past had left off.

When, nearly fifty years later, Griffith Jones inaugurated a series of Circulating Schools over 250,000 people, half the population of Wales, were taught to read using William Morgan's Bible. The language of that Bible also influenced spoken Welsh with the result that the language grew and did not fragment or die away. Within a century of the Protestant Reformation, the Welsh people had a Bible in their own language, a language that would survive and grow, thus ensuring that every Welsh-speaking Welshman owed a deep and very real debt to William Morgan.

Bishop Morgan

In 1595 William Morgan was appointed Bishop of Llandaff and immediately proceeded to revise his Welsh Bible. At about this time, he also published his translation of the Book of Common Prayer. In 1601 he moved to St Asaph in North Wales where he was appointed Bishop.

Despite his success as a writer and translator, William Morgan died in 1604 a relatively poor man. He received no payment for his great work, nor did he expect any. His grave is unknown but a memorial in the grounds of St Asaph Cathedral marks the achievement of the man who translated the Bible into Welsh.

THE LAST INVASION OF BRITAIN

The Pencaer Peninsula, where 12 French soldiers were captured.

Ask any casual passer-by for the date of the last invasion of Britain and the reply will probably be '1066.' If asked to try again, he or she might just venture '1688.' Both answers would be equally wrong. The last invasion took place in February 1797 when 1400 members of the French Legion Noire descended on the Pencaer Peninsula near Fishguard. They were an ill-assorted, desperate group of villains, many of them convicts who had been kept in chains until the invasion fleet sailed, the rest being the worst soldiers from every regiment in France. But for a brief period they had the whole of Britain at their mercy as panic spread across the country.

Led by a 70-year-old American called William Tate, the original aim of the Legion Noire was to provide a diversion for another assault on Ireland. The Irish plan failed but, regardless, Tate and his army left Brest with a view to causing chaos on the British mainland. Their original target was Bristol but contrary winds caused the fleet to head for the Welsh coast instead.

Detail from The Last Invasion Tapestry, kept at the Town Hall Fishguard (© Elisabeth Cramp).

When the Legion Noire approached the port of Fishguard on February 22, they were met by a single shot from the town fort. The French turned back and landed instead on the rugged rocks nearby Carreg Wastad Point – which was just as well as the fort had only three rounds of ammunition and the shot that had greeted the French had been a blank! Nevertheless, by late in the evening most of the French troops were ashore and the invasion had begun.

To defend Fishguard were just 190 part-time Fencibles, commanded by Lieutenant Colonel Thomas Knox. And next day, faced by overwhelming odds, Knox decided to withdraw towards Haverfordwest, leaving the town of Fishguard at the mercy of the French.

For two days the French soldiers, most of them half starved and mutinous, roamed the hills to the north of Fishguard. In theory they were supposed to be gathering supplies and transport. In practice they were

Gelli, a party of Welshmen met a group of French and opened fire. When the smoke cleared one Frenchman was dead and the others took to their heels.

Sometimes the encounters were more than a little ludicrous. At Brestgarn Farm, a drunken Frenchman stumbled into the house looking for food. Hearing what he took to be the click of a musket being cocked, he turned and fired through the face of a grandfather clock! The undoubted hero of the episode, however, was town cobbler Jemima Nicholas who marched onto the Pencaer Peninsula and, single handed, captured twelve French soldiers. They were probably drunk and frightened but that does not detract from the courage of her actions.

Faced by mutinous soldiers and Cawdor's relieving force, General Tate had no option but to surrender, the document being signed at what is now 'The Royal Oak' public house in the centre of Fishguard. Tate's invasion had lasted three days but in that time so great was the panic across the country that the Bank of England almost ran out of money. For the first time the Bank was forced to issue promissory paper notes for £1 and £2.

more intent on finding whatever alcohol and food they could lay their hands on in the farmhouses of the region.

As a relieving force of part-time soldiers and sailors under Lord Cawdor marched towards Fishguard, a number of skirmishes took place around the town. At one cottage a Frenchman demanded food. While he was eating, the householder crept up behind him and smashed him over the head with a chair. In a field below Carn

The Legend of the Welsh Women

There is a Pembrokeshire legend that Lord Cawdor persuaded local women in their red shawls and tall black hats to march around a hill so that the French would think they were soldiers. Believing themselves to be outnumbered, says the legend, the French promptly surrendered. Sadly, there is little truth in the story.

Welsh women certainly joined Lord Cawdor's advancing force and they were there in great numbers when Tate and the Legion Noire surrendered. Yet there is no record of Cawdor ever asking women to pretend to be soldiers and the real reason for the surrender was not that Tate was outnumbered, simply that his troops were out of control and he could do nothing with them.

Iwan Bala's striking composite image of three archetypal Welsh women, which includes Jemima Nicholas.

THE REBECCA RIOTS

Aberystwyth toll gate reconstructed at the Museum of Welsh Life, St Fagan's.

On May 13, 1839, as the skies above Efail-wen in Carmarthenshire began to turn dark, a group of men with faces blackened, all dressed as women, marched towards the village toll gate. Within a few moments the gate had been smashed and, as quickly as they had gathered, the mysterious rioters disappeared into the countryside.

That 1839 attack was the first in a series of disturbances that lasted until 1843, disturbances now known as the Rebecca Riots. There were numerous causes. In the early years of the nineteenth century, small farmers in west Wales were hit hard by the economic climate. A series of wet harvests, combined with an increase of over 60% in the population – and the levying of high rents by the largely English-speaking landlords – meant that discontent in the countryside was high. Taxes such as those raised by the 1834 Poor Law Amendment Act to pay for the building of workhouses caused more serious disgruntlement.

However, in the main, the rioters vented their anger on

Brett Breckon's visualisation of the Rebecca rioters.

the toll gates which proliferated across Wales. Turnpike trusts had been established to repair and maintain the road systems, tolls being levied to pay for the work. By the middle of the century, the gates had become too numerous – there were, for example, no fewer than eleven different turnpike companies operating around the town of Carmarthen – and the tolls far too high. To move livestock to and from market and to bring in essential materials like lime and cattle food had become prohibitively expensive.

One of the methods of meting out social justice in Wales was by forcing miscreants to ride the *ceffyl pren,* a wooden horse, through the streets of the town. Blackened faces and cross-dressing were part of the ritual, both to hide the identity of the people involved and because men dressing as women symbolised a world that had been turned upside down. The origin of the name Rebecca is not so clear. Legend says it was because one of the early

In the months that followed, several rioters were transported to Australia, others imprisoned, and the Government was forced to call a Commission of Enquiry to explore the grievances. As a result, in 1844 all the turnpike trusts within each shire in South Wales were amalgamated and tolls on the vital commodity of lime reduced by half. Rebecca had won her victory.

A school badge commemorating Rebecca (Beca).

leaders, Twm Carnabwth, borrowed his clothes from Rebecca of Llangolman but it could also relate to a verse from Genesis which talked of Rebecca and her seed 'possessing the gates of those which hate them.'

Between 1839 and 1843, the Daughters of Rebecca burned workhouses and toll gates across south-west Wales and even attacked the home of tithe agent Rees Goring Thomas. A march by 2,000 people into Carmarthen on June 19, 1843 culminated in the ransacking of the town workhouse, and dragoons charging the mob. Two months later, 3,000 rioters aired their grievances at Mynydd Sylen in Pontyberem.

No single mastermind behind the riots has ever been identified although Hugh Williams, a radical lawyer and Chartist from Carmarthen, has sometimes been credited with this role. In the main the attacks on the toll gates and workhouses were uncoordinated.
They were often the result of local disputes and therefore led by a wide range of individuals.

The blinding of a toll keeper's wife in Cardiganshire during one attack, and the death of Sarah Williams, the aged gatekeeper at Hendy, in the autumn of 1843, saw much of the popular support for the movement fall away and there was great debate within Rebecca's ranks between those in favour of violence and those opposed to it.

The Daughters of Rebecca

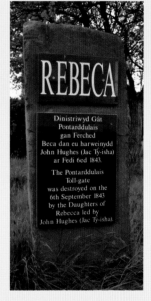

Such was the concern about the Rebecca Riots that *The Times* newspaper sent a reporter, Thomas Foster, to find out about the troubles. His sympathetic reporting outlined the grievances of the farmers and he was accepted by the rioters, even being invited to a secret meeting of Rebecca at Llandeilo.

Despite the sympathy of the London papers, John Hughes, John Hugh and David Jones were sent to Van Diemen's Land after the attack on the Pontarddulais toll gate in September 1843. Other men to find themselves transported included Dai Cantwr and Sioni Sgubor Fawr, both of whom favoured the violent approach and both of whom apparently laughed in the face of the judge when sentence was pronounced.

INDUSTRY
AND UPRISING

Until the middle years of the eighteenth century, industry in Wales was small-scale and the workforce part-time – men would toil in the fields during harvest and move on to local foundries and coal mines when agricultural needs were not so great. From the 1850s onwards, however, fuelled by the needs of war and by improved production techniques, there came an unprecedented demand for iron, copper and tinplate. Wales was ideally placed to provide these commodities.

By the 1860s, the Parys and Mona copper mines on Anglesey were employing over a thousand men while the quarries of Blaenau Ffestiniog and Llanberis had made Welsh slate the envy of the world. A new tinplate industry was established at Pontypool and Thomas Williams set up a copper-smelting plant near Swansea, thus beginning a process that would make the name of the town synonymous with the industry. From the port of Swansea, square-rigged sailing ships journeyed all over the world with their cargoes of precious metal.

The Seven Years War which began in 1756 meant that

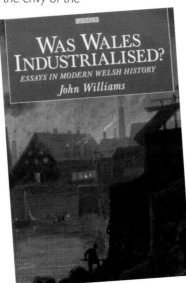

Two industries in decline: Diffwys Cason (slate) and Trawsfynydd (nuclear).

imported iron supplies were suddenly no longer available. When investors realised that all the raw materials needed to produce the metal were also available in the Principality – iron ore, limestone, coal and wood – there was an immediate rush to the South Wales valleys. Men like John Guest, who ran the Dowlais works near Merthy Tydfil, and Richard Crawshay of Cyfarthfa became famous as Welsh iron masters – yet they, along with Francis and Samuel Homfray from Penydarren, were actually Englishmen who had come to Wales as investors. And what an investment they made. The ironworks of South Wales were so successful that by 1820, just five years after the end of the Napoleonic Wars, they were

WAS WALES INDUSTRIALISED?
ESSAYS IN MODERN WELSH HISTORY
John Williams

and it was the 1830s before coal from South Wales began to be used as a domestic fuel in the great houses of the capital. Then came steam ships and railway trains. As the Royal Navy and the new railway companies began to use more and more coal, mining became an industry in its own right, rather than simply an adjunct to the smelting of copper and iron.

Men were needed to fuel the industrial boom and in the second half of the nineteenth century the Rhondda valleys, in particular, witnessed what can only be described as a 'coal rush.' Before 1850 there were just 1,000 people living in the Rhondda; by 1910 there were over 150,000. The results were squalid living conditions as families rushed to find work in the mines and create new lives for themselves in the houses that had been hastily thrown up along the valleys' sides. Poor water supplies, primitive sanitary arrangements and general overcrowding resulted in regular outbreaks of diseases like cholera, typhus and typhoid. Within the space of twenty years, green valleys were turned black with soot and grime as slag heaps littered the hills and the angular shapes of pit winding gears began to point like accusing fingers into the sky.

producing almost half of all Britain's iron exports.

Yet it is for coal that Wales is best known. The earliest reference to the use of coal in Wales dates from 1248 but it was 1695 before Humphrey Mackworth actually began to use it to smelt copper in the area around Neath. In the eighteenth century, coal was largely reserved for the smelting of iron

In the industrial centres of Wales, people worked long hours in dreadful and often dangerous conditions. Wages for the men – and, initially, women and children too – might have been better than they had received on the farms but they were still low and were often paid in tokens that were only usable in the company shops, the truck shops as they were known, where the prices were high and the quality of food was often

Crawshay Bailey's Ironworks at Nantyglo by J. P. Gastineau.

questionable. It was inevitable that discontent would, sooner or later, rear its head.

The Merthyr Riots of 1831 began when a mob ransacked the building where court records of debt were stored and twenty people were killed in the fracas. The authorities sent in a detachment from one of the Highland regiments to restore order and when a soldier was stabbed in the back, Richard Lewis, Dic Penderyn as he was known, was accused of the attack and later executed in Cardiff jail. Dic was innocent of the crime but the affair provided Wales with her first industrial martyr.

The Chartists brought a different and more complex set of problems for the mine and foundry owners. The Chartist movement had been created in the 1830s to seek a charter of political reform which, it was hoped, would sweep away all the inequalities and bad conditions that working people had to endure. The Chartists were idealists but idealists with an aim and a mission.

On November 2, 1839, the Welsh Chartists planned a march to Newport where they intended to hold a demonstration. Hundreds of workers from places like Merthyr, Blackwood and Blaenavon gathered together and made their way to Newport. Feelings, however, were running high and when marchers and soldiers clashed outside the town's Westgate Hotel, a full-scale battle broke out. Ten men were killed and the Chartist leaders – John Frost, Zephaniah Williams and William Jones – were sentenced to transportation for life.

Following the failure of the Chartist Rising at Newport, the movement fell into disarray. The Chartist ideal was kept alive for another twenty years but, with its leaders divided over strategy and tactics, never again did it manage to achieve the

The unacceptable face of industrial society. The Aberfan Disaster, 1966.

John Frost, Chartist Leader

WELCH CHARTIST MARTYRS!

ZEPHANIAH WILLIAMS.   JOHN FROST.   JONES, THE WATCHMAKE

A local businessman, John Frost had always been interested in politics and eventually became Town Mayor of Newport. Elected to the Chartist Convention in 1838, he was a moderate in his approach and tried hard to keep the more extreme members of the movement in check.

Frost was involved in the Chartist Rising of November 1839 and, along with Zephaniah Williams and William Jones, was originally condemned to death for his part in the affair. The sentence was later changed to transportation. In Australia, Frost eventually became a school teacher before being pardoned in 1854. He spent some time in America and returned to Britain, to a hero's welcome, two years later. He died in 1877, aged 93.

cohesiveness it had possessed before 1839. Yet the Chartists had shown that working-class men and women could be politically aware and their legacy provided the inspiration for thousands of trade union leaders and politicians in the years to come.

Despite the efforts of the Chartists, conditions in the industrial areas of Wales continued to be dire in the extreme. Increasingly, coal became the main industry of the country. By 1891 South Wales was producing thirty million tons of coal a year – by the peak year of 1913 that figure was up to 56 million tons, over one fifth of the total British coal production.

It was not until the nationalisation of Britain's coal mines in 1947 that conditions really improved. Now, with coal seams petering out and cheaper fuel becoming available from abroad, there is virtually no mining in Wales. The iron and steel industries have also become mere shadows of their former selves. It is hard to know if the Chartists and those who worked in the industries in the nineteenth century would be glad or sad.

THE WELSH NOT AND THE BLUE BOOKS

Education was not compulsory in Britain until the passing of Forster's Education Act in 1870. Prior to that the upper classes had their great Public Schools, paupers and delinquents had use of Industrial and Reformatory Schools, but for most people there was little provision. In nineteenth-century Wales, a limited degree of education for the working classes was provided by Sunday Schools and voluntary establishments run by the National (Anglican) and British (Nonconformist) Societies.

The rapid industrialisation of Wales and the riots and disturbances that broke out in the middle years of the century caused alarm in government circles. Many felt that the existence of a separate language in the country was one of the contributing factors.

In large parts of Wales – although the extent of its use has lately been questioned – schools used the 'Welsh Not' as a means of forcing children to speak English rather than Welsh. A piece of wood, inscribed with the letters 'WN', was hung around the neck of any child found speaking Welsh. He or she could only pass on the 'Welsh Not' to another child heard speaking the language and the unfortunate person possessing the 'WN' at the end of the day was given a sound thrashing by the teacher. Such a system not only prevented children using their native language, it also actively encouraged traits such as lying, tale telling and spying on others.

Use of the 'Welsh Not' may have been less widespread than originally thought but there is clear evidence of its use in Carmarthenshire, Cardiganshire and Meirionnydd. As the schools at the time were voluntary establishments, it is unlikely that headmasters would have introduced such a policy without the tacit approval of parents. However, despite their concerns about the Welsh language, use of the 'Welsh Not' was never government policy.

What the government did do was appoint a commission to enquire into the state of education in Wales. When the report, in its traditional blue covers, was published in 1847 it created a furore and immediately went down in Welsh folklore as The Treason of the Blue Books.

The report was written by Messrs Lingen, Symons and Vaughan Johnson, English barristers, assisted by a number of Anglican clergymen at a time when Wales was a hotbed of Nonconformism. None of them spoke Welsh yet the report was virulent in its attack on the standards of education provided. Unfortunately, the commissioners did not stop there. They went on to deplore the ignorance and depravity of the Welsh people, calling them lazy and immoral. Much of the problem, they said, was due to an inveterate use of the Welsh language. Things would only improve, boomed the commissioners, with the introduction of English-language teaching for all children.

The 'Welsh Not' was mentioned in the Blue Books of 1847 when inspectors called it both arbitrary and cruel. The practice was not endorsed by the report but it continued in use, albeit it in a sporadic way, for the next twenty or thirty years. The Education Act of 1870 created a network of Board Schools which, in due course, were absorbed by the new County Councils and thanks in no small measure to the influence of men like O.M. Edwards, Chief Inspector of Schools in Wales, instruction in Welsh became the norm for elementary schools in Welsh-speaking areas. A decline in the number of Welsh speakers continued for the first half of the twentieth century but it was due as much to the industrialisation of the country as it was to the use of instruments like the 'Welsh Not'.

Sculpture of O.M. Edwards and his son, Sir Ifan, at Llanuwchllyn.

The Treason of the Blue Books

There was no doubt that some of the commissioners' comments about the state of education in Wales were justified. In the town of Pembroke Dock, William Morris discovered the teacher, Miss Slocomb, plastering a wall while her charges slept or fought amongst themselves at the back of the room. The children were cold and dishevelled and Miss Slocomb was almost entirely ignorant of even the most basic principles of education.

The National School in Pembroke Dock received unqualified praise, however. The same inspector felt that the lure of good jobs in the nearby Royal Naval Dockyard was a real impetus for hard work by pupils and teachers alike.

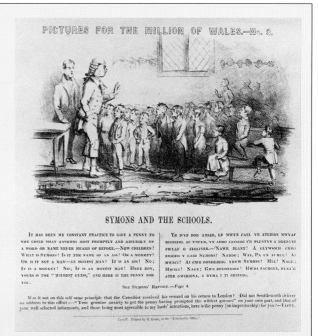

WALES AND TWO WORLD WARS

The First World War began on August 4, 1914. Welsh chapels were initially opposed to the conflict; many sermons were preached on the theme that this was a continental war and that Britain should remain neutral. Newspaper accounts of supposed German atrocities in Belgium soon changed that stance and, within a month, the churches and chapels of Wales had put their not inconsiderable weight behind the war effort.

Welshmen could sympathize with the oppression of a tiny country like Belgium and thousands rushed to enlist in Kitchener's New Army. In Wales, as in the rest of Britain, there was a desire to get out to France 'to do one's bit' because, as everybody knew, the war would undoubtedly be over by Christmas!

This sudden surge of patriotism was shown in the proliferation of sentimental poems that quickly began to appear in the pages of local newspapers across Wales:-

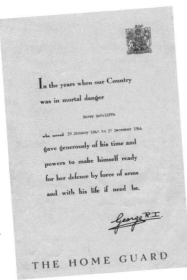

In the years when our Country was in mortal danger

Harry Ratcliffe

who served 30 January 1941 to 31 December 1944 gave generously of his time and powers to make himself ready for her defence by force of arms and with his life if need be.

George R.I.

THE HOME GUARD

The King's gratitude.

May God defend our country
Is the cry of everyone;
This war is forced upon us,
Welcomed by none.
(C. Allen, Penarth, September 1914)

It was not just Welsh civilians who took up their pens; soldiers also began to turn to verse. Such efforts were not great poems but they did express the soldiers' feelings:

When first they fought at Ypres
By the early morning light,
The way they stormed the German trench
Was indeed a glorious sight.
(Corporal Oscar Foote
of the Guards, 1914)

While soldiers fought in Flanders and France, back in Wales people found that the state, now on a war footing, was interfering in their lives in a way never before thought possible. Coal mines and railways were placed under government control and, as the war went on, food was rationed and price control rigidly enforced. The demand for Welsh coal was huge and wages in the industry rose rapidly.

When conscription was introduced in 1916, it was violently opposed by the miners and this, together with a growing opposition to the capitalists who were reaping huge profits out of the war, helped push them into the arms of the waiting Labour Party. A deeply-rooted and highly effective left-wing militancy took hold of the Welsh valleys so that when the war ended in 1918 and the soldiers finally came home, a vastly different country awaited them.

The inter-war Depression years were not easy with Welsh coal, iron and steel industries suffering a severe slump and thousands being thrown out of work. Only with the coming of the Second World War in September 1939 did, ironically, a measure of prosperity return to Wales.

The outbreak of the Second World War was not greeted with the same mass hysteria that had marked 1914, people being content to simply wait for their call-up, but there was still a solid and unified desire to stop the aggression of Hitler's Nazi Germany. The civilian population of Wales was heavily involved in the war almost from the beginning, not only serving in the armed forces but also working in armament factories and suffering some of the heaviest bombing attacks of the war.

The government had originally planned to evacuate nearly three-and-a-half million children and, in some instances their mothers as well, to the safety of rural Wales for the duration of the war. In the event only thousands, rather than millions, took up the offer, most people preferring to keep their children close to them, whatever the dangers. For those who did make the journey there was, in the main, a warm welcome but the trauma for young children, ripped away from family and familiar surroundings, was immense:

Pembroke Dock under attack.

The Swansea Blitz.

Great Fire of London in 1666. Cardiff and the South Wales valleys were also subjected to heavy bombing but it was the three-day blitz of Swansea in February 1941 that really brought home the effects of war to the Welsh people. In three days and nights of incessant attacks the centre of the town was flattened and hundreds of civilians were killed.

Unemployment in Wales fell sharply during the war: by 1944 over 30% of the population was engaged in war work of some type. And the nature of the workforce, with many men serving in the forces, changed dramatically. In 1939 only 90,000 Welsh women went out to work. By 1945 that figure stood at well over 200,000. Many women found employment in the armament factories at places like Bridgend, Hirwaun, Glascoed and Caerwent.

In the coal industry, however, there was a desperate shortage of miners and the government was forced to conscript men to work underground rather than in the armed forces. The Bevin Boy scheme put thousands of young men into the Welsh mines, giving them experiences of life they had never even dreamed about.

Despite the social and environmental problems brought by war, living standards certainly improved in Wales and between 1939 and 1945 the wages of working men and women were doubled. It was some small crumb of comfort.

We got on the train and mum and dad were very upset. 'Try and stay together,' Mum said, 'please stay together.' On the train young Jean was sick – she was just a baby really. And Esther wasn't happy either. We were all really emotional but, being the eldest, I was thinking 'Where are we going? When are we going to get there?'

(Violet Cropper)

It had been thought that the Germans would never manage to bomb Wales but after the fall of France in 1940, large parts of the country suddenly came within range of German bombers. A raid on the oil tanks at Pembroke Dock in August 1940 caused the largest fire seen in Britain since the

News Chronicle

No. 30,881   TUESDAY, MAY 8, 1945   ONE PENNY

TODAY IS V DAY

Churchill speaks at 3 p.m., the King at 9; Today and tomorrow are national holidays

TODAY IS V DAY AND A PUBLIC HOLIDAY. TO-MORROW IS V DAY PLUS ONE AND IS ALSO A PUBLIC HOLIDAY.

THIS WAS ANNOUNCED LAST NIGHT IN THE FOLLOWING OFFICIAL STATEMENT:

"It is understood that in accordance with arrangements between the three Great Powers an official announcement will be broadcast by the Prime Minister at three o'clock tomorrow afternoon, May 8.

"In view of this fact, tomorrow, Tuesday, will be treated as Victory in Europe Day and will be regarded as a holiday. The day following, May 9, will also be a holiday.

"His Majesty the King will broadcast to the peoples of the British Empire and Commonwealth tomorrow at 9 p.m.

"Parliament will meet at the usual time tomorrow."

THANKSGIVING SERVICE

It may be that shortly after the Premier's announcement the Commons will go in procession to St. Margaret's to give thanks, headed by the Speaker, Col. Clifton Brown.

forces, at the order of Grand Admiral Doenitz, has today declared the unconditional surrender of all fighting German troops."

ANNOUNCED BY GERMANS

The surrender had been signed at 2.41 a.m., in the small red schoolhouse near Rheims which Gen. Eisenhower uses as his headquarters.

There were three other broadcasts during the day:

The announcement by Doenitz that on May 4 he had ordered all U-boats to return to their bases;

The declaration by the German-controlled Prague station that the Germans there would ignore the surrender; and

Boehme, commander of the Wehrmacht in Norway announced that his troops, too, would have "to bow to the dictate of our enemies in the interests of the German

They waited in Piccadilly Circus, but had nothing to cheer

The crowds which waited for the announcement that did not come in Piccadilly Circus last evening. Time was 6.5 p.m. A few people are grouped round Eros. Others are drifting towards the Underground stairs. There are few flags. More pictures on Back Page

LONDON PUT OUT ITS FLAGS AND WAITED | Allied fleet off

Welsh Political Leaders

David Lloyd George had been Liberal MP for Caernarfon since 1890, a man renowned for his powers of oratory and belief in improved schemes of social welfare. During the First World War he became, first, a highly efficient Minister of Munitions and then Minister of War. In December 1916 he became Prime Minister, an appointment that was greeted with great enthusiasm throughout Wales and his charisma and power guided Britain to ultimate victory in the war.

Aneurin Bevan was a miner who was elected as Labour MP for the steel and iron producing community of Ebbw Vale in 1929. Despite being opposed to government policy throughout the Second World War, he became Health Minister in the Labour government during the last months of war. Under his guidance the foundations of the National Health Service were laid and a programme of slum clearance begun.

THE NATIONAL ASSEMBLY OF WALES

Cardiff Bay

The years after the end of the Second World War witnessed a growing sense of Welsh identity. Yet, to begin with, there was much ambivalence towards Wales and all matters Welsh from Clement Attlee's post-war Labour government. Attlee dismissed the appeal for a Secretary of State for Wales and it was not until 1951 that the new Conservative government created the position of Minister for Welsh Affairs and added it to the duties of the Home Secretary. A Secretary of State for Wales, along with the Welsh Office, eventually became a reality in 1964.

Plaid Cymru, the Welsh Nationalist party, had been founded in 1925 but it was the unexpected election of Plaid's leader, Gwynfor Evans, as MP for Carmarthen in July 1966 that brought home the realisation that Wales was a country with an identity of its own and could no longer be conveniently ignored.

The Kilbrandon Commission was set up in 1969 to look at the possibility of devolution for both Wales and Scotland, its recommendations forming the basis for the 1974 White Paper 'Democracy and Devolution'.

Gwynfor Evans

The Wales Act was placed on the Statute Book in 1978 and, despite the proposed body having very limited powers, a site was chosen for the new Assembly. However, in a referendum held on St David's Day 1979, the Welsh public voted against the concept of devolution by the huge majority of four to one. It was a setback for the supporters of nationalism and the idea of devolution disappeared from the Welsh political scene for over ten years.

The idea did not go away, however. In the 1990s it resurfaced, to some extent due to concerns felt about all-powerful quangos like the Welsh Development Agency which were controlling vast amounts of Welsh Office spending. Not only that, for ten years before 1979, Wales had been represented in the cabinet by a Secretary of State who did not even represent a Welsh constituency! Then, championed by Ron Davies, the new Secretary of State for Wales, a second referendum was held on

The Assembly

Although the Assembly has limited legislative and fiscal powers, it retains the right to pass secondary legislation in many areas. This has resulted in several significant achievements. These include the scrapping of all NHS prescription charges for people living in Wales, a revolutionary decision that will have major effects in the years ahead.

Members are elected under a mix of proportional representation and single member constituencies where a traditional 'first-past-the-post' system applies.

September 18, 1997. The referendum was supported by Labour, Plaid Cymru, Liberal Democrats and by many church groups and trade unions but was opposed by the Conservative party. At the end of an emotional night, and by a tiny majority of 6,721, with just 50.3% of the votes cast, Labour's proposals for devolution were accepted by the Welsh electorate. The Assembly was duly formed under the Government of Wales Act 1998.

The new Assembly was located in Cardiff, the capital city of Wales, and consisted of 60 members, led by a First Minister. The Senedd – Welsh for Parliament – building was finally finished eight years after it was first announced, a landmark building that is located on the waterfront of the old Cardiff docks. Designed by Sir Richard Rogers, the building cost £67 million, more than five times more than had been originally planned, and was only completed after

a two-year break for a dispute between the Welsh Assembly Government and Richard Rogers. Queen Elizabeth II formally opened the building on March 1, St David's Day, 2006.

Elections to the Assembly are held every four years and the vote of 2003 saw the formation of a body where half of the seats were held by women, probably the first time that open, democratic elections have ever produced equal representation for women. Following a by-election at Blaenau Gwent in 2003, women members actually became the majority.

The Welsh Assembly was the first elected government body to meet in Wales since Owain Glyndŵr called his Parliament at Machynlleth in 1404. As such, its creation was, and remains, a major moment in Welsh history.

Owain Glyndwr's parliament building at Machynlleth.

Acknowledgements

The author and publishers gratefully acknowledge the following sources of images:

BBC: 1, 37 (centre and bottom); Ken Day: 2-3 (top), 16 (bottom), 17 (bottom); Castell Henllys: 2 and 3 (bottom); National Eisteddfod: 4 (bottom); Anthony Griffiths: 5 (top), 13 (top), 16 (top), 19 (top); Cardiff Library: 5 (bottom); The County Council of the City and County of Cardiff: 6 (top), 14 (top); Martin Cavaney: 6 (bottom), 17 (top); Suzanne Carpenter: 7 (top); Welsh Tourist Board: 7 (bottom); Steve Benbow/PhotolibraryWales: 8 (top); National Library of Wales: 8 (bottom), 11 (bottom), 22 (bottom) 33 (bottom); Hywel Dda Heritage Centre: 9; Cadw: 10 (top), 12 (top); Gawain Davies (bottom); Ivy Bush Hotel, Carmarthen: 11 (top); Roger Turvey/Gomer 11 (bottom); Dean and Chapter of Westminster Abbey: 13 (bottom); Mick Sharp: 14 (bottom), 15 (top); The Princess Gwenllian Society: 15 (bottom); Welsh Tourist Board: 18 (top); Terry Beggs: 18-19 (bottom); S4C: 20 (top); Margaret Jones and National Library of Wales: 20 (bottom); Marian Delyth: 21 (bottom); Hugh Olliff: 22 (bottom); Dyfed Elis-Gruffydd: 23 (bottom); Fishguard Invasion Centre Trust Ltd: 24 (top); Ray Wood: 24-25 (top); Iwan Bala: 25 (bottom); Aled Rhys Hughes: 26-27; Brett Breckon: 26 (bottom); Jeremy Moore: 28-29 (top); National Museum of Wales Department of Industry: 29 (bottom); Western Mail & Echo: 30; Ron Davies: 31 (bottom); Tegwyn Roberts: 33 (top), 39 (bottom); Harry Radcliffe: 34 (bottom); West Glamorgan Archive Service: 36; Ken Davies: 38 (bottom)

Front cover: Tery Beggs/Henry Jones-Davies (Cambria)/Welsh Tourist Board/Gary Evans

Back cover: Marian Delyth/National Library of Wales/Peter Lord